Hell Yes!

Two Little Words for a Simpler, Happier Life

Elizabeth Cogswell Baskin

**Andrews McMeel
Publishing, LLC**

Kansas City

09 10 11 12 13 SDB 10 9 8 7 6 5 4 3 2 1

ISBN-13: 978-0-7407-7919-0
ISBN-10: 0-7407-7919-2

Library of Congress Control Number:
2008935740

Book design by Holly Camerlinck
Illustrations by James Yang
www.andrewsmcmeel.com

Attention: Schools and Businesses
. . . .
Andrews McMeel books are available at quantity discounts with bulk purchase for educational, business, or sales promotional use. For information, please write to: Special Sales Department, Andrews McMeel Publishing, LLC, 1130 Walnut Street, Kansas City, Missouri 64106.

You do too much.

I don't know you, but I'll bet you're busier than you really want to be. You might be the CEO or the office intern, a stay-at-home parent or a part-time student, a doctor, a lawyer, a butcher, a baker, or a candlestick maker, but my money says you're overcommitted.

Do you really want to be one of those people who are always overwhelmed? Imagine instead being highly productive yet more relaxed. Imagine waking up excited about what's on your calendar, going through your day feeling energized and joyful, or even having nice, roomy holes in your schedule.

The trick is to do the things that are on your true path, and skip the rest. "Follow your bliss," said Joseph Campbell, the esteemed twentieth-century psychologist. "Do you," says Russell Simmons, the CEO of hip-hop. "Choose what makes you feel good," says Abraham, a group of spiritual entities channeled through Esther Hicks. And as Alan Cohen, author and speaker, says, "You only have to decide one thing. If it's not 'Hell yes,' then I don't care what it is."

Before you commit to anything—a meeting, a lunch date, a favor for a friend, a volunteer opportunity, a marriage proposal, or even another piece of pie—use this simple measurement to weigh your options.

If it's not a "Hell yes!" then it's a "Hell no!"

This one sentence acts like a razor to cut away the clutter. It compels you to say no to the opportunities that fall into that dangerous gray area of things that don't excite you but aren't exactly heinous either. Start noticing when you find yourself thinking, "I don't want to, but I should." Or, "Well, he seems like a nice guy and I hate to turn him down." A common mistake is

to say yes to something you don't really want to
do because you think it won't take much time.
(It always does.) Or to agree to a commitment on
some date way out in the future, because you think
your schedule will surely be much less jam-packed
by then. (It never is.)

Maybe you think saying no isn't nice, or that it's
being irresponsible. You worry about letting people
down, or making someone mad. Guess what? That
person is probably not that into you. If you say
no, he or she will just go down the list and ask
someone else. And maybe someone else would love
the opportunity because it really is on his or her
true path. The truly responsible choice is to not do
things halfheartedly. You would be shortchanging
the other person involved, not to mention yourself.

That's not to say you should do only the fun stuff.
If your kid breaks his arm at school, then hell yes
you're going to head straight for the emergency
room, even though you're not looking forward to
it. As author Chellie Campbell says, the trick is to

stay purposely undercommitted. She knows she's more creative when she has time to just putter around. And she knows she's happier, too.

When you begin practicing the "Hell yes!" rule of thumb, you will notice some shifts. The obvious one is you'll spend more time on things that truly matter to you and less time on the ones that don't. You'll also create space for more of the good stuff—from creative ideas to spontaneous lunch dates to the ability to say yes to some exciting new opportunity when it comes your way. But the shift that's perhaps the biggest relief is you won't spend untold time and angst trying to figure out what you want, from whether or not to buy a pair of shoes you see on sale to whether or not to take that big job offer.

If it's not a "Hell yes!" then it's a "Hell no!" Can these two little words really make your life simpler and happier?

If you ask me, "Hell yes!"

Here's the secret to a simpler, happier life.

Before you put one more thing
on your calendar,

before you agree

to take on a new project,

before you say yes to an invitation,

Yes!

before you buy something,
· ·

even before you eat something,

ask yourself one simple question:

Is it a

"Hell yes!"?

If it's not a
"He l yes!"
· ·

then let your answer be

"Hell no!"

This one simple question

serves as the sharpest razor,

swiftly and completely
cutting away anything
in the gray area.

It immediately frees you
from all the things you agree to do
because you don't stop to think

about whether you really want to do them.

Or because it's a good cause,

or she's a nice person,

or it won't take that much time,

or it's something you probably should do.

Most important, this question

keeps you on your true path.

Because your true path is marked

by the things that light up for you.

You move down your true path by doing

the things that feel exciting and fun to you.

The things that make you say,

"Hell yes!

I want to do that!"

That's not to say you might not be afraid.

Or feel like you won't be good at it right away.

Feeling scared is one way you know

you're stretching yourself into more growth.

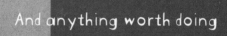

And anything worth doing

is worth doing badly in the beginning.

Sometimes you might feel pressure to take on a

"Hell no!"

because you feel bad saying no.

You worry about disappointing

the person who asked.

But isn't it a little egotistical
to think that you might be the only one
who could fill the bill?

If you say no, that person will just move down the list

and ask someone else.

And maybe the next person will say,

Consider that you might be making room

for someone else to do something

that's on his or her true path.

Maybe you're afraid the opportunity

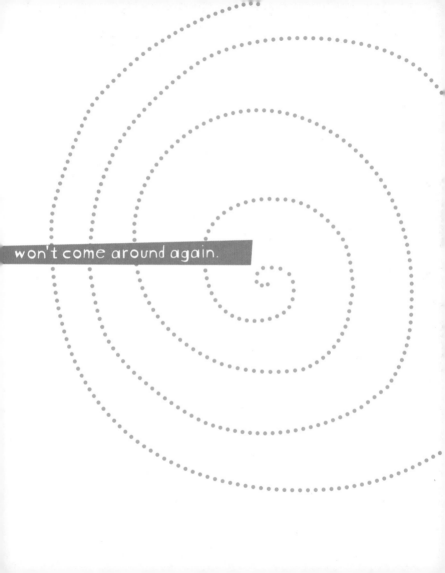

won't come around again.

It might not.

But every day is filled with new opportunities.

Choice upon choice.

More choices than we can ever say

"Hell yes!" to.

If you're still waffling,

ask yourself one more question:

What will it cost to say yes?

How much time, energy, money,

or just plain wear and tear will it cost you?

If you have to think that hard about it,

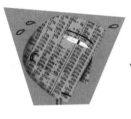

you might be thinking too hard.

One of the most efficient aspects of the

"Hell yes!/Hell no!"

rule is this:

If it's not a clear

"Hell yes!"

then you don't have to figure out

what else it could be.

You don't have to weigh out
all the pros and cons of the maybes.

Because if it's not a

"Hell yes!"

then it's a

"Hell no!"

It's that simple.
. . . .

When you start saying no to things

that aren't exciting to you,

a beautiful thing happens.

Your calendar becomes nice and roomy,

which helps you feel nice and relaxed.

You also create space in your calendar to say yes to the last-minute opportunities that do get you excited.

If you schedule every day to the gills,

you limit your ability to respond

when something important comes up.

And something always comes up.

Create space in your life.

And watch how your life responds.

You'll wake up in the morning and say

"Hell yes!"

to your day.

And when you look back on your life,